Galápagos Joy

poems by

Paul Stroble

Finishing Line Press
Georgetown, Kentucky

Galápagos Joy

Copyright © 2023 by Paul Stroble
ISBN 979-8-88838-108-3 First Edition
All rights reserved under International and Pan-American Copyright Conventions. No part of this book may be reproduced in any manner whatsoever without written permission from the publisher, except in the case of brief quotations embodied in critical articles and reviews.

ACKNOWLEDGMENTS

Some of the poems in "historia" first appeared in my chapbook *Backyard Darwin*, Finishing Line Press, 2019.

Paul Stroble teaches at Webster University and Eden Theological Seminary. He has published poems of history, science, faith, and Midwestern memory in previous collections for Finishing Line Press.

Publisher: Leah Huete de Maines
Editor: Christen Kincaid
Cover Art: HMS Beagle at Tierra del Fuego, https://en.wikipedia.org/wiki/File:HMS_Beagle_by_Conrad_Martens.jpg
Author Photo: Jeannie Liautaud Photography, LLC
Cover Design: Elizabeth Maines McCleavy

Order online: www.finishinglinepress.com
also available on amazon.com

Author inquiries and mail orders:
Finishing Line Press
PO Box 1626
Georgetown, Kentucky 40324
USA

Table of Contents

mi oración 1

I
viaje 2
buenos días 3
plantas 4
aves 6
geología 9
tortugas 10
iguanas 12
insectos y arañas 13
felicidad 14

II
historia 16

III
criaturas endémicas 23
exploración 24
muerte y vida 26
creación de Dios 28
en el avión 32

Notes 33

mi oración

  El Panecillo,
Holy Virgin of Quito,
   Madonna clothed in the sun,
I'm not Catholic,

  but I pray at this altar
witnessed by the golden wall.

Aren't we as children,
claiming a homely place for
   discovery and surprise,

eager to learn names
of creatures, rocks, plants, and trees,
   wonder deeply?

  Might I find God's Kingdom
as a child, curious,
   a natural scientist?

I.

viaje

    1535,
Fray Tomás de Berlanga,
        Bishop of Panama,
    discovered these islands and
saw little evidence for God's favor,
    no future for man, little fresh water,

    birds too foolish to flee,
tortoises amble by the tens of thousands,
cacti, black and pale lizards,
dark boulders form the shoreline as if
    God had showered stones....

    1684,
talk in Pirate to William Dampier
    hydrographer who chronicled
so much new,
    stopped at these islands,
wrote of the tameness of the birds,
    and the pleasing meat
        of tortoises;
the sparseness of the islands
        and the South Winds.

    1835,
and Darwin wrote upon arrival,
Black basaltic stones,
thrown into most rugged waves,
covered by sun-burnt brushwood,
    Nothing could be less inviting.
And the tortoises, the birds....

buenos días

      Our intrepid group
can't wait to start. We have our backpacks, cameras,
phones, sunscreen, boots, water, snacks.

      How did Darwin even live in this heat,
without summer shorts?

      There's record cold back home.
Don't put your tongue on the Arch….

      Stifle yourself, damn rooster,
it's 4 AM …

            but that's your time,

and all the darkness creatures,
rice rats and geckos and hawks
      in endemic balance

7 o'clock breakfast,
Ecuadoran coffee (black for me).

      Introduced species,
a kitty cat turns in the warmth
           for belly rubs.

plantas

   The cat's claw and club moss,
milkwort herb and goat's head,
Galápagos tomatoes;

   our photos of cactus blooms
as they greet the morning sun.
     Purslane, succulents
that feed the land iguanas and
the crawling coastal insects.

   Be happy for life,
not an imagined lushness
   from saltwater waves.

But the mangroves, too:
   niches that lodge
local species.

   Sing *Joy to the World!*
island mistletoe,
   tiny wild poinsettias
down the path toward
   a spring and rare fresh water.

———

   To love plants
as Darwin did:
     the older man's
stay-at-home happiness at his
     careful attention.

His six botanical books look loved
in Murray green
   upon my shelves back home:

   the natural
circumambulation of twining life;

more vigorous plants
when cross-fertilized, become
   more vigorous still.

　　　　Insect murder! The
sundew, its sticky leaves, most
sagacious plant.

　　　　Darwin timed plants' growth rates,
watched them as they slept,
described their clever contrivances
　　　　unneedful of divine adjustment.

　　　　The master Humboldt knew, too:
plants bless both mind and heart,
　　　　even bless with moral freedom.
Plants migrate the earth,
　　　　seeds lodged in the winds,
　　　　in the wings of birds,
the boots of those who wander.

　　　　Take care! Sapiens comes in
tramping.

aves

        The eternal waves,
as if they were Time itself.

        Blue-footed boobies
dive as a flock arrowlike
        into the sea's darker blue.

(I LOVE BOOBIES shirts
        in the boardwalk stores can't do
them justice: no big surprise.)

        Herons and egrets, finches;
hungry penguins need
the currents to bring small fish.

Pelicans' unique profile,
        shaded by saltbush, but
Dinnertime! and it flies away.

        Mockingbirds
rather than finches first piqued
        Darwin's homesick interest:
the way their species
        are found on particular
islands but not the others.

Red-billed tropic birds
live on the open ocean,
        breed on land—they sense the time.

Is the mother bird late?
Here is her egg in the brush:
        baby albatross to be.

Watch the woodpecker finches use tools:
twigs and cactus spines
        to pull insects from the bark,

and Galápagos doves,
their brown, black and pink feathers,
        with their familiar call for mates.

How happy to see
vermilion flycatchers
        in a Palo Santo tree,
the tree's pleasing scent
        that lingers like church incense
while the bird gives me side eye.
———

Audubon, Wilson, Brewer,
        Chapman, LaBastille:

to devote your life to birds!
    I wanted to, in my childhood yard,
watching the mockingbird
        that helped our antenna
                pull in four channels;
        the berry eater
                that bombed me when I was small.

In the brush of San Cristóbal
        a male frigate bird
fills its red pouch,
        knows its ritual for a mate.

        Subvert the Patriarchy!
for both mates work on nests,
        both care for the young.

        Stunning in flight,
they glide over water.
oil glands too unproductive
        to keep feathers from being
soaked. What would you do?

You'd forage, small fish churned up
        by currents, dolphins.
And you'd steal, from smaller birds.

God has not died for the birds.
        Thus Yeats. But their theft
does not break a commandment…

Watch out!
 frigate poop
comes calling.

geología

The Nazca Plate moves quickly,
    four centimeters a year.

    The young islands
still form, living volcanos.
  1825, 2000 feet of flame from
    the peak of Fernandia,
shower of molten stone
    that heats the waves to 65° C.

Eruptions happen still:
    since 1535 over 50,
though not here on Española,
    oldest island eroded,
black, abundant lava stone.

    Was that a tremor?...

    Charles Lyell,
his studies of rocks
    and strata, soil, and fossils,
the ways the earth has been formed.

    Science and Bible:
fossils were left from older,
    destroyed creations,
which fit well with Genesis.

Now Lyell: the earth
was always as it is now,
    and alters very slowly:
uniform change over the vast epochs.

As the *Beagle* crew
mapped out each island
    under Captain FitzRoy,
        Darwin
gathered volcano data, which were the oldest,
which igneous stones had formed,
    which were worn down from the sea.

tortugas

        Anticipation!
great tortoises, well cared for in
        their captive breeding program.

      We will be long dead
by the time these young ones
reach old age, even middle age.
          Even Lonesome George—
the last of the subspecies
of Pinta Island tortoise—
      was perhaps only
a hundred, yet unable
      to be successfully bred.

———

      All the box turtles
I took to school show-and-tell—
      easy to carry, quite cool—
then released, each one
          into the backyard again,
their day in the human world.

      Those distinctive shields,
ribs, spine, and pelvis modified,
beautiful carapace.
      I really believed
they came out of their shells
      at will, as in the cartoons.

      I'm sorry to you,
dear pets I didn't know to care for:
newt, horned toad, hamster,

      finally buried
in the backyard. Even at a slow pace,
the turtles
      knew to escape me.

———

            If you were at sea—
say, a pirate—and knew that
tortoises could provide meat
            for lengthy sea trips,
how many would you store up,
            though you risked
                        the whole species?

(A koan: could you
            climb atop a tortoise and
                        ride it as if a surfboard?
Darwin did. But we
            must go to their safest place,
                        which is to say, before man.)

            Two male tortoises
on San Cristóbal
            rear their heads,
                        their beaks wide open.

            Which will back down first?
Does a tortoise feel macho,
            or ashamed?
                        I'm projecting.

iguanas

        On the boulders
of Española,
        slaughters of iguanas chill
(so to speak), sun themselves
            toward 40° C
then enter the cold water.

      So ugly even
their mothers won't stick around,
            but they easily choose mates.

—

The beholder's eye
      sees the fondest beauty,
           godlike in its open heart.
Take John Muir, for instance:
      beautiful children of God
are the Florida crocodile.

      Darwin thought
females are born with an aesthetic sense
      for choosing their mates.
Wallace added:
           beauty brings us joy, useful
not just for finding partners.

—

Please keep bobbing. Damn!
      Student with stopwatch must count
the times iguana's heads bob: homework.

          On San Cristóbal,
I saw a tall prickly pear
      with a resting cactus finch.
A pad falls, and soon
      an iguana eats it, spines
and all.
      No indigestion?

insectos y arañas

      A green hawkmoth parks
at my hostel door. Careful!
      It dares you to walk with care.

      Painted ladies
in motion: red, black,
      orange wings
like the fritillaries.

      Numerous ant species,
some uninvited, some endemic.

      I'd rather not see
an orb web spider, less
      to walk into its web,
even less to meet
          endemic kinds
of scorpions under rocks.

Say *bright black bee*
      five times fast:
a carpenter bee
      zooms by for its daily work:
common island sight,

      Xylocopa darwini.
I show it respect.

felicidad

        The sea lion groans
like a worn-out soul,
        like him horizontal on a bench.
Would you ask it to share space?

        Dinner on the boardwalk,
local cuisine,
        fun conversation—
these mojitos, strong AF—
piña coladas, red wine.

        Can anyone talk to our waiter?
Cuentas separadas, por favor!
        But he runs away!
Where's he going?
Here he comes,
        shleping all that Bacardi.

Our poor friend! *You could
open your own restaurant
        and call it The Nasty Shack!*
All she did was to
order cuy, cooked on the open spit.
        It's delicious!

———

        *The nature of things,
the Greeks' curiosity,
should not concern the Christian.*
        Thus, St. Augustine.

*The beginning of all sin
was curiosity.*
        Thus, Bernard of Clairvaux.

        But the wisest of teachers
may preach most foolish notions.
Learning is a joy,
        with experiences, risks.

Darwin used all his senses.
Armadillos taste like duck;
        that rare Christmas rhea;
    a scrumptious brown rodent;
fluid from tortoise bladders:
       check off the creatures Darwin ate.

He'd taste anything
for science, culinary
     flavors hitherto untried.

———

   Shopping.
We cleaned that lady
out of her pretty bags at
    Ciudad Mitad del Mundo.

Stop at this store, too:
    pills for altitude sickness,
Dramamine for the boat rides.

Back at the San Cristóbal boardwalk,
rub Charles' nose
    as you would Springfield's Lincoln.

The Beagle model, nearby,
    Darwin in his suit.
Give him bunny ears, a hug.

II.

historia

In the welcome indoor air,
       I scroll through histories
on my device:

       Darwin's influences,
Lamarck, Whewell, and Malthus,
Bacon and De Candolle;

       and Banks, with
the Endeavor crewmen, landing on
Tahiti…

       Bates, laying gunpower
to deal with the ants…

       Linnaeus, exuberant joy
for order,
              counting on
      his traveling helpers…

       Cuvier: take care!
              species lost
do not return…

       Hooker, around
the globe to discover plants…

       Buffon: influencing
his generation…

       loyal Asa Gray,
American supporter.

       I read
Webster of the Chanticleer,
               Nuttall in Arkansas;
      Bates, Spruce and Wallace
          the Amazon buds.

      I miss my antique books
back home.
      But I brought
my 1890 *Origin* in a plastic bag.

———

The Humboldt Current,
ocean stream—and the master's
epochal exploration,

     lonely Tegel child
inspired by Captain Cook and Forster
    to travel,

    five years exploring
South and North America;
data for his future books
    adored in Europe and
in America;
        his courage
    to attempt Chimborazo
then turning its life
    to art: *Naturgemälde!*
science fills the heart with peace,

    beauty of data,
measurement and art, cosmos—
as we learn to keep it safe.

    Would Charles have been here
without Humboldt's narratives?
Now I almost adore him…

             And Jefferson,
who sent out Lewis and Clark, tapped
the master's Western knowledge.

             And Zebulon Pike,
his plagiarized Humboldt maps
             gave him his own mountain fame.
                          And the great Southwest,
so beautifully described
             in *Essay* everyone read?

             America's drive for land,
coast to coast, in a hurry.

             (Remember our stop
for interstate pancakes, close
             to the home of James K. Polk:
the trip to Space Camp
             and our daughter's own voyage
studying the last frontier?)

             Till there came the time
to open my soul and kneel
at Ecuadoran altars.

             I, too, drove cheerful
through the postcard scenery
             of Manifest Destiny.

———

             I read of Darwin's
years on the Beagle: that long
seasick journey set the stage
             for all else he did,

and at sea he devoured
Humboldt, Lyell's *Principles*
             smelling of damp timbers—
took his careful notes
and collected specimens
             shipped back to England.

He would write, *Not hopes,
fears, but truth as reason permits us
to discover it.*

Species fixity,
such a cherished idea;
the religious hurled brickbats
                    at the best-seller
Vestiges of Creation,

       so anyone else
who was pro-evolution
must have his facts in order
                    and his theory
as airtight as possible,
thus Darwin's 20-year wait.

       Struggle in nature
for existence leads to the
preservation of useful
                    derivations of
form and structure, instinct and
         adaptation,
                    death and life.
The balance may tip
so that a creature survives,
              thus more,
         varied progeny.

       If God designs, why
would God create similar
species among these islands?

       Humboldt knew, too,
change occurs on earth, climate,
         and in organisms, too;
famous Tennyson,
       *Nature, red in tooth and claw
With ravine, shriek'd against creed.*

　　　　Charles' main idea
gave him debilitating
　　　　　anxiety, stomach pain:
species develop
through descent, adaptation,
　　　　　　which is true for humans, too.

　　　　　　　Humans the apex
of creation? God's image?
　　　　　Stability of species?

He followed his doubt
but he told friend Hooker,
It's like confessing a murder....

———

　　　　　1858 in England:
announcement of
　　　　　what became the paradigm:
selection explains
　　　　　　varieties of species:
brilliant Darwin and Wallace.

　　　　Lyell, Huxley, Gray,
and Hooker pushed acceptance
of Charles' long brewing theory:
　　　　Huxley called himself
"Darwin's bulldog," *Origin's*
blunt and battling advocate.

　　　　　　Hooker gave Darwin
friendship and encouragement.
He was always for Darwin
　　　*the one living soul
from whom I have constantly
received support, sympathy.*

　　　　　Darwin gained priority.
But take heart, prolific Wallace! You were
　　　　never drawn as a monkey,

and your books grace my shelves.
———

*There is a struggle for existence
leading to the preservation
   of profitable deviations of structure
or instinct.* Darwin's insight.

    Finch with cracking bills,
finch that eat grubs: most famous
    of his observations.

Don't they evidence
    natural adaptation,
and not of divine design?

    What is the mechanism
        by which traits
pass to parents' offspring?
    Darwin did not know Mendel's
work on plant heredity—few did—

    but Pangenesis
was his provisional name
for what he had long observed.

Now, we know of
    genetic transmutation,
and groups expand in
    ecological niches
that before had been empty.

It's proven: finches' beaks do alter
    in observable time,
    with available resources!

There is variance
    among species:
coloration, sounds, and habits,
wonders of creatures across
    biogeography.

Beautiful research: evolution in genes
        and genera,
genetic markers,
        transposable elements—
                McClintock's jumping genes—
        CRISPR-Cas9 technology ….

Tell the doubter this,
and shout it from the hills
        and from the pulpits
        and in the legislative halls:

*"Nothing in biology makes sense
except in light of evolution."*

III.

criaturas endémicas

      Pop quiz:
what are the indigenous,
endemic species found on these islands?

      Don't look for
native sparrows, jays, blackbirds,
woodpeckers, or hummingbirds.

      Introduced cattle, horses,
dogs, cats, pigs, mice, and others

      but few native types,
rice rats, hoary bats, red bats:
that's it.
      No amphibians.

      Paleontologists
look for lava tubes
           for fossil evidence.

Lizards, tortoises,
      snakes have thrived and multiplied.
How and when did they get here?
      A reptilian Kon-Tiki in eons past?
Keep working on your theories.

exploración

       Next day:
eternal waves,
pahoehoe and aa lava,
            splashing tide.

(*I'm nobody! Who are you?*
Are you nobody, too?
       wrote Emily Dickinson)

On board, a woman
with full diving equipment
       chats, smiles with the good crew,
trades phone numbers with one.
       (Later, she got off the plane
at Guayaquil.)

       Panama Current,
Equatorial Counter-current,
       the Humboldt Current:
ocean forces in
balance with land for climate
       and marine ecosystems.

I scan the sea for Pacific green sea turtles:
       only females come ashore
for egg laying time.
Imagine a whole lifespan
       eating, sleeping in the waves.

       Española's shore:
watch the force of water blow
       through the volcanic crevice,
an exhalation
       like a bituminous chest,
magma in Poseidon's biome.

       Color on black rock:
Sally lightfoot crabs—orange shell,
       red legs, their purple eyes—

         hang effortlessly
                    to stones in surf, scavengers
         always busy. Nom nom nom.

                    Few coral reefs here,
         they don't thrive in cool water,
                    but there are anemones,
         coral relatives
                    that feed on plankton as do
         the spiral Christmas tree worms.

                    Snorkling the bay, and
         an eel makes its way:
                    that's a morey…
         Classic awful joke
         as I'm floating
                    face-first in the clear water.

                    A hieroglyphic hawkfish or ten;
         yellowtail surgeonfish, sergeant major,
                    blue-chinned parrotfish;
         water colors of blue and
         yellow, green and pink and red….

                    Starboard commotion:
         two rays make mighty splashes
                    as they mate at the surface.

                    You know what they say:
         birds do it, and bees do it.
                    Genetic inheritance.

muerte y vida

        Today, on Isla Lobos,
a dead seal, starved when
            the mother could not return.
Alas, poor Yorick,
        we said, in contemplation
of the hot, bleached and clean skull.

        How can we not
joke of death? Memento mori,
        we blunt its sting with humor,
yet reel from stories
        of human horrors—like those
of these islands' history,

        cruel prison, scandals,
strange tales,
        strong-willed baroness
and her lover disappeared.

        We know that Darwin
found satisfying answers
            in the greatness of nature
and he shed belief across his years.
Let each hope,
        he writes, believe what he can.

            Darwin could not see
evidence of divine care:
        the cruelties of nature:
ichneumons' larvae's
        unlucky host;
any cat after a mouse.

        And yet, Darwin's praise:
there is grandeur in this view of life,
beautiful new life evolves…

        from famine, death,
the most exalted object
        which we are capable of

*conceiving, namely,
the production of higher
      animals, always follows.*

creación de Dios

Night thoughts.
      I turn science and faith
like a Rubik's Cube™
              and love the puzzle.

      Huxley coined the word
agnosticism. He wrote,
Follow reason where it leads!

      True—and the world's faiths
acknowledge death, suffering,
trust and courage in response,
      God's closeness to all:
the lilies—more glory than
      Solomon—the small, frail birds.

      Islam: Allah's most
beautiful names: Creator,
the Merciful, Sustainer
      of all that exists,
Subtle, Just, Beneficent,
      All-Wise, Bestower of forms....

      The bodhisattva Avalokiteshvara
looks on us with compassion.
      We cling to the thought
that death should be calm, correct.
Free us from our clinging!...

      The Nataraja:
Shiva's ecstatic dancing
moves out the old for the new,
      like earth's volcanos
that wipe the land clear of life,
creating new soil, dark, rich ...

      The Bible: God provides
through life, death and renewal,
      takes the side of all creatures,

             the rhythms of
sustaining, redeeming, sanctifying.

God's mountains tremble,
             creatures drown each other out
with wordless acclamation.

       Read Psalm 104:
humans are put in place
             in the Earth's systems, with birds
and beasts and the fish,
             living things both small and great
innumerable are there.

       And open faith's heart
to the *Naturgemälde*,
Nature as a living whole;
                    the moral freedom
gifted by naturalists;
science, art, and Self hold hands.

Is it more noble
             to develop and transform
from earlier kinds of life,
interrelated,
             or to be related as
created by God? (Or both?)

             Imago Dei,
our Spirit-breath is plant-based:
             their life cycles let us breathe.

             Imago Dei,
alone of life reaches out
to know, predict, theorize.

             Matter has emerged
as persons!
             reflecting upon

    order and design, discovering
            codes in every living thing.
Life's mosaic is A C T G.

        Incarnate Reason,
the first born of creation,

the Son of Man suffers.
        The pain of flesh is felt
by Divinity.

        Form of encoded order,
            the Infinite Life,
con- or transubstantial
        with creatures of atoms, genes.

            Human paradox:
we're of the natural world,
yet pained by our finitude,
        grieved by suffering,
confused and downcast by death,
        unsure of the infinite.

        God constantly creates,
clears away, continues work,
nearer than nucleotides,
        Other than the world,
immanent, embracing chance,
            freedom and variety.

        Wallace: infinite intelligences
            guide that which is.
Selection's centrifugal governor,
        life's self-corrections.

Again, Darwin's praise,
        As our planet spins,
wonderful, endless life forms
have been, are being evolved.

You know, O Mortal:
  lose any portion
of the interconnection,
   and life adapts or dies

   There are no islands,
but teeming, terrestrial
    zones of life's varieties
like these far over
   trackless seas, our friendship songs
of pleasant exploration.

    Love these creatures, then,
for stained glass sanctuaries,
from Life and Light
    come all life.

en el avión

        I forgot to find
the Southern Cross. It was there,
but I was searching toward Earth
        as anemone swayed,
old tortoises grumbled
        at fellow slowpokes,

        frigate birds scouted craters,
boobies danced blue,
        cold water sprayed on us
            from the salty,
stone-showered shore.

        Black basaltic stones,
thrown into most rugged waves,
        covered by sun-burnt brushwood.
Nothing could be less
inviting, Charles wrote in his journal,
        so prematurely.

———

        El Panecillo,
Holy Virgin of Quito,
        Madonna clothed in the sun,
you dance on the snake
        at the altar of Francis
in apocalyptic sky.

        Praise be to the Lord
of ten thousand billion suns
        and the creatures of one cell,
of daily delight
        the more we learn and connect
and write up our research notes.

May we return here
someday, see more islands,
        give Darwin
bunny ears again.

"Joyful is the one who finds wisdom,
who acquires understanding."

Notes

This story is based on my March 2019 visit to the Galápagos Islands with the Webster University BIOL 1020/1021 spring break trip, hosted by the Universidad San Francisco de Quito. I joined the group as a Webster adjunct faculty in another department. My deepest thanks go to Dr. Nicole Miller-Struttmann and Dr. Stephanie Schroeder for leading this group; to Kris Hickman for giving me a Spanish translation herein; to the whole group of wonderful students; and to Andrés Esteban León and Nabih Iván Dahik Quiroz of USFQ for their guidance, in Ecuador and on the islands. We visited San Cristobal, Isla Lobos, and Española. Dr. Struttmann commented during the trip, "children are natural scientists," unwittingly providing me a direction with some of these poems. I also thank Dr. Kim Kleinman, who has led me into new areas of the history of science; Dr. Victoria Brown-Kennerly, for helping me understand genetic research (and for reminding me of the word "mosaic"); and Dr. Mary Lai Preuss, who told me about Barbara McClintock.

The reflections herein were not part of the course but represent my personal enjoyment of and reflection about the islands. Any factual errors are mine alone.

Many thanks also to Dr. Tom Dukes, who made possible my dream of writing poetry; Dr. Charles Barnes, Dr. Andrea Scarpino, Jane Ellen Ibur, Heathen, the Webster Groves Starbucks; the Novel Neighbor Bookstore; the St. Louis Poetry Center; Stacey Stachowicz and her family; and especially Beth and Emily.

The following books helped me identify species that we saw and to understand aspects of the islands, or otherwise interested me. John Hess, *The Galápagos: Exploring Darwin's Tapestry* (Columbia: University of Missouri Press, 2009); Michael H. Jackson, *Galápagos: A Natural History, Revised and Expanded Edition* (Calgary: University of Calgary Press, 1993); Mark Newman, *Galápagos: In Darwin's Footsteps* (Smashwords Edition, 2012); Steven Rosenberg, *A Naturalist's Guide to the Galápagos Islands*, 2nd edition (Apple Books, 2014); Alan Moorehead, *Darwin and the Beagle* (New York: Harper & Row, 1969); Niles Eldredge, *Darwin: Discovering the Tree of Life* (New York: W. W. Norton & Co., 2005).

Specific quotations (or close paraphrases) are as follows:

mi oración

I have conflated two statues of the Virgin of Quito: the tall aluminum statue

Virgin of El Panecillo, and the one that decorates the main altar at Quito's Church of St. Francis. The latter inspired the former.

viaje

The Fray Tomás de Berlanga quote is from "A letter to His Majesty, from Fray Tomás de Berlanga, describing his voyage from Panamá to Puerto Viejo, and the hardships he encountered in this navigation," April 26, 1535. John Woram, *Human and Cartographic History of the Galápagos Islands*, http://www.galapagos.to/TEXTS/BERLANGA.HTM Accessed August 24, 2019.

The Darwin quote is from Charles Darwin, *A Naturalist's Voyage: Journal of Researches into the Natural History and Geology of the Countries Visited during the Voyage of H. M. S. Beagle Round the World* (London: John Murray, 1889), 373.

aves

The William Butler Yeats quotes is paraphrased from his play "Calvary," in M. L. Rosenthal, ed., *Selected Poems and Two Plays of William Butler Yeats* (New York: Collier Books, 1962), 194-201.

iguanas

Slaughter is the collective noun for a group of iguanas. An iguana mother never returns to her nest of eggs, which, contrary to my joke, has nothing to do with ugliness. Baby iguanas are equipped to survive on their own from birth.

felicidad

On the discouragement of curiosity within the Christian tradition, see Joyce Appleby, *Shores of Knowledge: New World Discoveries and the Scientific Imagination* (New York: W. W. Norton & Company, 2013), 3-5.

On Darwin's adventurous eating, see, for instance, Jessie Rack, "Dining Like Darwin: When Scientists Swallow Their Subjects," Aug. 12, 2015. https://www.npr.org/sections/thesalt/2015/08/12/430075644/dining-like-darwin-when-scientists-swallow-their-subjects Accessed June 7, 2021.

historia

Prussian naturalist and polymath Alexander von Humboldt (1769-1859) inspired numerous naturalists, writers, and artists with his long research voyages and his comprehensive vision of the universe, *Cosmos*. His travel journals enchanted many, including Darwin, who wrote in 1832, "I formerly admired Humboldt, I now almost adore him." Humboldt's data-filled drawing of the Ecuadoran mountain Chimborazo—he called artwork *Naturgemälde*—was very influential. Humboldt also published his *Political Essay on the Kingdom of New Spain* (1811), which caught Americans' imagination. In 1804, Humboldt met with Thomas Jefferson—who had sent out Lewis and Clark, who departed from St. Louis in 1803—and provided the president with data about the trans-Mississippi West in advance of Lewis and Clark's reports. Jefferson also appointed Zebulon Pike, who journeyed from St. Louis to the Rockies with a plagiarized map of Humboldt's. In time, Humboldt's descriptions of Mexico precipitated U.S. interest in Mexican territories, and ultimately the Mexican War during the presidency of James K. Polk. See Aaron Sachs, *The Humboldt Current: Nineteenth Century Exploration and the Roots of American Environmentalism* (New York: Penguin Books, 2006); Laura Dassow Walls, *Alexander von Humboldt and the Shaping of America* (Chicago: University of Chicago Press, 2009).

"Not hopes, fears…" Charles Darwin, *The Descent of Man*, and *Selection in Relation to Sex* (New York: D. Appleton & Co., 1897) 619.

"famous Tennyson." The well-known verse from Tennyson's poem "In Memoriam A.H.H." (Canto 56) is, "Who trusted God was love indeed/And love Creation's final law/Tho' Nature, red in tooth and claw/With ravine, shriek'd against his creed."

"Like confessing murder…" C. Darwin to J. D. Hooker [January 11th, 1844], in Francis Darwin (ed.), *The Life and Letters of Charles Darwin*. Vol. 2 (London: John Murray Press, 1887) 23. Darwin Online, http://test.darwin-online.org.uk/ content/frameset?pageseq=1&itemID=F1452.2&viewtype=text Accessed July 26, 2019.

"Nothing makes sense…" Theodosius Dobzhansky, "Nothing makes sense in biology except in light of evolution." *The American Biology Teacher* (1973) 35 (3): 125–129. https://doi.org/10.2307/4444260 Quoted in Brian Charlesworth and Deborah Charlesworth, "Darwin and Genetics, *GENETICS* November 1, 2009 vol. 183 no. 3 757766; https://doi.org/10.1534/genetics.109.109991 Accessed July 10, 2021.

Some of the lines in this section were adapted from my previous book *Backyard Darwin* (Georgetown, KY: Finishing Line Press, 2019).

exploración

The Emily Dickinson quote is from T. W. Higginson and Mabel Loomis Todd (eds.), *Poems of Emily Dickinson*. Second Series (Boston, Roberts Brothers, 1891) 21.

muerte y vida

"Let each hope…" Darwin to Asa Gray, May 22 [1860], third paragraph. The quotation is: "Let each man hope & believe what he can." *Darwin Correspondence Project*, http://www.darwinproject.ac.uk/letter/DCP-LETT-2814.xml Accessed December 17, 2017.

"And yet… from famine, death…." This is a paraphrase of the last paragraph of Darwin's *Origin of Species*.

creación de Dios

"Huxley coined the word…" Thomas Huxley, *Christianity and Agnosticism: A Controversy. II. Agnosticism* (NY: The Humboldt Publishing Co., 1889), https://archive.org/stream/agnosticism00variuoft/agnosticism00variuoft_djvu.txt. Accessed December 20, 2017.

"and open faith's heart…" Humboldt's data-filled drawing of Chimborazo, *Naturgemälde* or "painting of nature," conveyed his philosophy of the wholeness of nature; the unity, variety, and interrelationship of all things; the model of nature as an organism rather than a mechanism. Andrea Wulf, *The Invention of Nature: Alexander von Humboldt's New World* (New York: Alfred A. Knopf, 2015), 88-93, 126-129.

"Matter has emerged as persons!" Arthur Peacocke, *God and the New Biology* (Gloucester, MA: Peter Smith, 1994), 121.

"There are no islands…" and "like these far over…" These make use of lines in Walt Whitman's poem *Passage to India*, section 8, and John Donne's famous saying, "No man is an Island," from his *Devotions Upon Emergent Occasions*, Meditation XVII.

"As our planet spins…" is from the last paragraph of Darwin's *Origin of Species*.

en el avión

"Joyful is the one…" is Proverbs 3:13.

www.ingramcontent.com/pod-product-compliance
Lightning Source LLC
Chambersburg PA
CBHW022123090426
42743CB00008B/974